Tarot

Thorsons First Directions

Tarot

Evelyne Herbin and Terry Donaldson

Thorsons
An imprint of HarperCollins*Publishers*
77-85 Fulham Palace Road,
Hammersmith, London W6 8JB

The Thorsons website address is:
www.thorsons.com

Published by Thorsons 2000

10 9 8 7 6 5 4 3 2 1

Text derived from *Principles of Tarot*, published by Thorsons 1996

Evelyne Herbin and Terry Donaldson assert the moral right to be
identified as the authors of this work

Editor: Jo Kyle
Design: Wheelhouse Creative
Photography by Henry Allen and PhotoDisc Europe Ltd.

A catalogue record for this book
is available from the British Library

ISBN 0 00 710331 X

Printed and bound in Hong Kong

Contents

Tarot

is an ancient system of divination using

a deck of illustrated cards

Tarot is...

What is Tarot?

The Tarot is something that functions on many levels.

On one level, it is a set of cards that portray a way of looking at the world. A way of making sense of the world, rather than an attempt to define and limit it.

   On another level, it is an approach to life, which enables each of us to move away from our own private realities towards the point of being able to have a multi-viewpoint.

   This is the primary purpose of the Tarot: to give us a set of windows through which we can look upon life. It has other qualities too:

- It is a counselling tool.
- It is a means through which communication – sometimes on a highly psychic or highly intuitive level – can take place.
- It is the means through which countless people over countless years have found a place to gain a resolution to the problems which have beset them.

How Tarot works

The Tarot works through synchronicity – in other words, the random patterns in which the cards seem to fall are part of a greater pattern within the cosmic scheme of things. This may seem chaotic to some, but not to those who seek to understand the nature of the causes of things; to those who have learned to look for causes which in turn give rise to effects.

This, then, is the function of Tarot: to facilitate our grasp of how things may be changed in the future through a deepening of our realization of what has happened in the past.

How Tarot can help

The Tarot has always held a great deal of mystery down through the ages, especially for those who have desired to become more familiar with its message.

It is a message – or a map – of how we may achieve greater fulfilment in our lives, through a balancing of the emotional aspects with the material. Not through a denial of either. Many people can't see a way out of their problems because they do not have an alternative point of reference from which they

can begin to see clearly what choices they do have. The Tarot reading can be a starting point for many.

Misguided notions

There are people out there who still cling to the outdated notion that to be able to read the Tarot you have to be born with a hereditary gift to do so. The truth is that the door of Tarot opens itself to all those who genuinely desire to understand its mysteries, and who would make positive use of the knowledge and guidance which they would receive.

Working with the cards

It is not so much what is 'in the cards', as what we ourselves are able to see in them. Depending on our knowledge, we will see representations of legends, tales from mythology, hints at 'secrets', and explanations of them as well.
To work with the cards is a bit like going to the gym – it will enhance whatever is latent within each individual, depending on the amount of effort and actual work done.

As we mentioned earlier, you don't have to possess a special gift in order to read the cards. By working with the cards though you will bring out your psychic potential, and activate it far more than you can imagine at this time. Thus, working with the cards will enable you to become far more intuitive about life in general, and more perceptive about yourself and others.

Historical origins

As to the historical origins of the Tarot, there are many different explanations. The actual Tarot as we know it today dates back to fourteenth-century Italy where we find a nobleman commissioning a hand-painted deck to commemorate the marriage of his daughter. But there are historical records to indicate the use of cards for divinatory purposes earlier than that.

We have always used symbols, in one form or another. Indeed, it is where we get the letters of the alphabet from, each of which at one time held a particular meaning. The Runestones, the Ogham, etc, all date back a lot further than the Tarot as such, although in one sense we might regard them as the earliest forms of Tarot, with their straight lines being marked on pieces of wood or stone to represent storm, harvest, war, protection, etc.

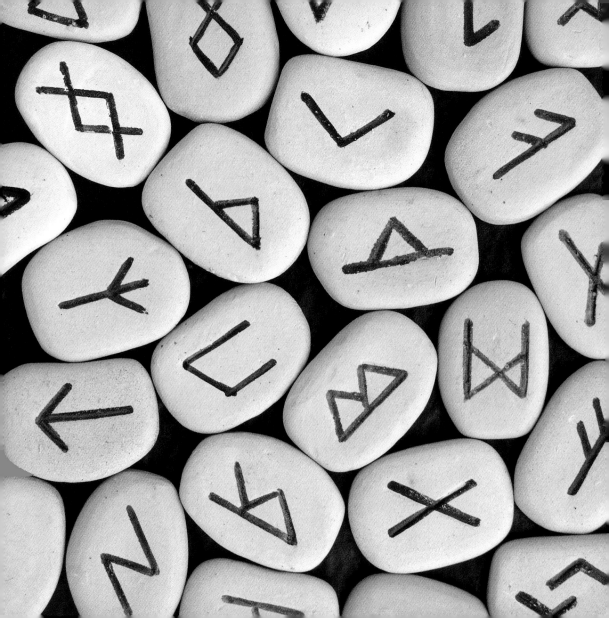

It is from the casting down onto the ground of these stones in ancient times that we have the phrase 'magic spell', because from the single letters which would be carved on each individual stone, the local 'wise person' would be able to spell (i.e. make out) the words or utterances of the gods which they believed protected them.

The word 'magic' is from the same root as the words 'image', 'imagination', 'magi'. It is therefore pointing us in the direction of achieving wisdom through the development of our ability to creatively visualize, to imagine. To put aside your preconceived notions, to let your intuition function with less restraint from your conscious mind, to become aware of your own limitations and to move increasingly beyond them.

This is the very essence of how to approach the Tarot.

The Cards Themselves

The structure of Tarot

The Tarot is divided into two sections – the Major Arcana and the Minor Arcana. The pictures contain references to folklore, mythology, legends, characters from history, and provide us with lessons which we can begin to apply in our own lives.

The Major Arcana

The Major Arcana consists of 22 cards. When you lay the cards out for yourself or for others and any of these cards come up, it will be showing the most important things that the querent (the person who is getting the reading; the 'questioner') is there to learn.

The sequence of the Major Arcana cards is listed below. Note that a number of variations on the sequence of the cards can be encountered, depending on the particular deck you are using.

0	The Fool	11	Justice
1	The Magician	12	The Hanged Man
2	The High Priestess	13	Death
3	The Empress	14	Temperance
4	The Emperor	15	The Devil
5	The Hierophant	16	The Tower
6	The Lovers	17	The Star
7	The Chariot	18	The Moon
8	Strength	19	The Sun
9	The Hermit	20	Judgement
10	The Wheel of Fortune	21	The World

The Minor Arcana

The Minor Arcana consists of 56 cards, which show different everyday situations, including 16 court cards (see below) which describe personality-types, or 'archetypes' – different people and influences that make up our lives.

   The Minor Arcana cards derive from our ordinary playing cards, and like them are divided into four suits: coins (or pentacles or discs), cups, swords and wands. Each of the suits are equivalent to a suit of a conventional playing card pack.

   Generally, the Minor Arcana cards are laid out to give the querent an answer to a question. They may not have an actual question, however, but may be interested in getting an overview of their life from what the tarot reading has to offer.

Coins are equivalent to Diamonds

Cups are equivalent to Hearts

Swords are equivalent to Spades

Wands are equivalent to Clubs

The court cards

The cards that indicate people are called the court cards. These are the kings, queens, pages and knights. They can show either situations, or actual people who are significant in the querent's life at the time of the reading. Traditionally, the cards represent someone of the same sex, i.e. kings show men, queens show women. It is worth bearing in mind, though, that a king, for instance, could also represent a woman who is in a position of authority, or heavily biased towards her masculine side, while a queen could represent a man who plays a nurturing role in the querent's life.

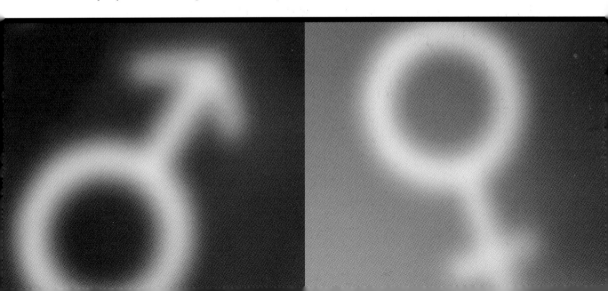

Long gone are the old associations between the court cards and 'dark-haired women' or 'blond, blue-eyed men'. This link may have been relevant at one time, but the world has changed since those times, and so have the meanings of the cards. These days, anyone can change the colour of their hair; with special contact lenses they can even change the colour of their eyes. The cards have more important things to do, more important messages to deliver than people's colouring.

****

Now we are going to look at the individual meanings and associations of each of the cards. We are going to start with the Major Arcana, and then go on to the Minor Arcana. Later on, we are going to show you how to do readings. Step by step we will show you how to make sense out of it all. The key thing is to enjoy it as we go along. Don't turn it into hard work!

The
Major Arcana

The Major Arcana follows the journey of the Fool towards
spiritual fulfilment. I have described each stage of this Journey,
card by card, and 'animated' it so that you can, if you wish, join
the Fool along the way.

The Fool

· THE FOOL ·

The Fool we see moving along Life's great road. He travels light, carrying nothing from the past except for a small bag of tools, keepsakes and necessities. He looks forward to the future without cares and worries, confident in what it will bring, and confident about his ability to meet it. You find yourself joining this character on his adventure. What do you want to get out of this experience?

The Fool teaches us that we have to go out there and experience life in full. Life is an exciting adventure. To know life, we have to seek our own truth, we need to expand our boundaries. The Fool's journey is here to emphasize our own individuality, not compromise it.

The Fool trusts what the universe has to offer. He has no fear. He does not worry about what he could have done or could have been. It is in the past. He creates his future now in the present time, not in the past or future tense. The Fool lives a simple life. Simplicity is the key to life!

Negative Aspects

erratic • naïve • rebellious • recklessness • uncommitted • unrealistic • lack of focus

Key Words

foolish • enthusiastic • unpredictable • versatile • spontaneous • unusual/different • taking risks

Suggestions

- Do something different or unusual.
- Keep your life simple.
- Know your fears.

The Magician

The Magician stands at his table, demonstrating his skills and techniques to passers-by. He calls out to you to come and see what he is doing. You stop and go to get a better look. You find yourself astonished at the cleverness of this man. How does he do these tricks? Is it sleight-of-hand, or some greater power? You find yourself quite unable to explain it.

The Magician teaches us about the role of communication, of developing our own ability to make ourselves clearly understood. We will develop through exercising our own minds and using reason.

He is there to remind us to be on our guard against blind faith, or even overwhelmingly strong emotions. Study, and the training of our minds will give us the chance to develop our faculties in a systematic manner.

He shows us how to communicate, how to sell our ideas, how to develop abilities and craftsmanship, how to solve problems, how to juggle with different things at the same time.

Negative Aspects

con man • dishonest • cunning/sly • volatile • argumentative • too intellectual

Key Words

communication • flexibility • dexterity • self-determined • thoughtful • dispassionate

Suggestions

- Learn to communicate effectively.
- Value knowledge and make use of everything you have learned.
- Be alert and aware.

The High Priestess

The High Priestess sits at the entrance to King Solomon's temple of Initiation. She is the guardian of the entrance to this new dimension of experience that you are about to enter. In her hands she holds a book – the Torah – which is a symbol of the explanation of life and its mysteries. You are about to enter this temple. Are you nervous? You should be, because your life is never going to be the same again! The High Priestess takes you by the hand and pulls back the veil that separates the outer courtyard from the inner, and thereby enables you to enter.

The High Priestess is the Goddess within. She is the feminine principle, the Yin, the receptive side. She represents intuition. She shows us that the path to realisation is reached by overcoming our own self-doubts, and by listening more trustingly to our own feelings and intuitions.

She is also synonymous with virginity or purity (the Virgin Mary, the Goddess Isis). In this instance, virginity would be the symbol of purity, i.e. in thoughts, feelings, desires, looks, words and gestures.

Negative Aspects

superstitious • inhibited • feeling mentally or physically impure • sacrifices • passive

Key Words

common sense • intuitive • psychic • inner wisdom • subjective • sanctuary

Suggestions
- Learn about flowers and gems and their healing powers.
- Respect yourself and others.
- Develop your intuition. Put some perspective in your life.

The
Empress

The Empress sits on her throne, and welcomes you into the garden in which she presides. Her domain is over nature, and all forms of growth and harmony. In the background are gentle running streams, trees rustling in the light breeze, and birds are singing. It is very idyllic. She invites you to sit beside her, and as you sit you feel the texture of the grass like a thick rug. She turns around and asks you if you have a wish. What do you say?

The Empress teaches us how to love, and she fills up our lives with feelings; of joy, happiness and contentment. She manifests and gives birth to what we love, desire and nurture. She is the goddess of love, mother goddess, earth goddess, goddess of fertility.

The Empress shows us how we can learn about our emotions and feelings through self-expression. She reminds us not to react too negatively to setbacks in life, but to keep going. We must also learn to stand up for our rights, and be aware of when others are manipulating and exploiting us.

Negative Aspects

too compromising • dependency • lack of assertiveness • too sensitive • dislike being alone

Key Words

empathy • compassion • wisdom • creative abundance • self-worth • family • pregnancy

Suggestions

- Cultivate your creativity (poetry, photography, etc).
- Give back your talents to the world in helping the community.
- Give love to everything and everybody.

The Emperor

The Emperor awaits your arrival. You enter his throne and the doors are closed behind you by his guards. He has something very important to say to you personally, otherwise one of his assistants could have dealt with you. He leans forward and in a whisper tells you about a forthcoming battle which he must face. Will you join forces with him?

The Emperor stands for leadership and self-determinism. He shows us how we can develop these qualities in our own lives.

The Emperor teaches us to develop through our own personal power. He teaches us not to be so reliant on others: we must follow our own instincts and impulses. We should not allow ourselves to become dominated or manipulated by others. The main areas we have to work on are our self-reliance and self-confidence. We will achieve happiness when we learn to value our own opinions and stand up for ourselves.

Negative Aspects

ruthless • intolerant • domineering • vain • aggressive • selfish • cowardly

Key Words

powerful • visionary • strong • ambitious • brave • self-sufficient • self-assured • inspiring

Suggestions

- Be true to your own goals.
- Be brave and confront problems.
- Struggle for your own independence.

The Hierophant

The Hierophant is the Grand Master of some secret society which you have stumbled upon. Are you going to join this secret group, or oppose them? Is what they are working towards good, or harmful for humanity? You make your decision, and the Hierophant reaches out and touches you between your eyebrows. Instantly you feel differently about your life. You see that he is the representative of an ancient mystical tradition that has borne the light of humanity throughout many ages of darkness and suppression, and you feel ennobled and special to have been chosen to join them.

The Hierophant is also known as the High Priest or Pope. This card shows us how to grow spiritually.

The Hierophant teaches us about compassion and charity. He helps others in a way that doesn't bring himself any direct benefit. He teaches us the lessons of persistence, loyalty, patience and perseverance in the face of opposition. He teaches us to respect the faiths and beliefs of others. The Hierophant's most important teaching is that 'by their fruits ye shall know them', in other words, a person's actions will speak louder than their words.

Negative Aspects

dogmatic • autocratic • conformist • immoral • orthodoxy • hypocrisy • indoctrination

Key Words

spirituality • rituals • charity • philosophical • revelation • ethics • tradition • marriage • community

Suggestions

- Explore new beliefs.
- Become a good listener.
- Make yourself available for charitable work.

The Lovers

You are in an open field and feel the warmth of the sunshine upon your skin. You notice that you are naked. In the distance you hear the sound of human voices, and then you see groups of people, some naked, some with garlands in their hair, making a procession towards you, dancing and singing as they move forward. From out of the melee the most beautiful man/woman comes towards you. There is a sense of destiny as you look at each other. This other person is waiting for you to take the initiative. Are you going to become lovers?

In the Lovers card we come across the whole dimension of love, attraction, desire and sexuality.

This card is very relevant in getting us to look at our problems in love and sexuality. When we encounter an obstacle, do we allow ourselves to remain blocked, or do we try to overcome the obstacle? Many people remain unfulfilled because they are unaware of the sacrifices that have to be made in order to find love. In order to experience what this card has to offer we have to be prepared to pay the price.

Negative Aspects

promiscuity • obsessive • emotional dependency • disliking the opposite sex • lack of commitment • too many expectations

Key Words

intimacy • emotionally secure • friendship • good rapport • faithfulness • same goals

Suggestions
- Be willing to give and receive love.
- Talk more openly to your partner.
- Don't approach your relationship with rigid rules or expectations.
- Be flexible and creative.

The Chariot

You are walking along a dusty road, when suddenly, from round a bend, you see a chariot moving at top speed toward you. The driver hasn't had time to see you, let alone take any action to avoid you. You dive to one side, and so narrowly miss the wheels of the speeding chariot. The driver pulls up his chariot and jumps down to see if he has hit you. He reaches down to help you back up to your feet. You are a bit shaken, but otherwise unhurt. The charioteer says something to you. What does he say? Does he offer to help you continue with your journey, or does he ask for your help in some way?

The Charioteer knows where he is going. In contrast, many people have lost their sense of direction and don't know where they are going in their lives. They have lost sight of their goals. Thus, the Chariot card is getting us to define our goals. This card also stresses the importance of living in the present, in the moment. The past will only entangle us.

   Another aspect of the Chariot card is about borders, demarcation lines and barriers. People have fences around their gardens and psychological spaces around their bodies. Without boundaries, we start taking liberties with other people's space and this leads to friction.

Negative Aspects

powerlessness • confusion • unable to complete any task • emotional • overprotective • lack of personal barriers

Key Words

purposeful • willpower • tenacity • exploring • nurturing • guarding • home sweet home

Suggestions
- Every day, be reminded of your goal.
- Draw boundaries when it is necessary.
- Learn to complete tasks.

Strength

We are walking through a wild mountain scene, in a jungle where the overgrowth has thinned out a little to make our passage easier. Through a clump of bushes we see a young man wrestling with a lion. The lion itself is huge, far bigger than any normal sized creature, but it is the man who captivates our interest more. He seems to radiate a power of some kind. We wonder what to do at this point in our Journey. Should we call out to him and introduce ourselves? Or should we play it safe and continue on our Journey and hope that he doesn't see us?

The Strength card is about inner strength, the ability to make change with our willpower.

It gets us to look at those areas in which we can effectively use our strength, or strengths. Each person has different strengths. Some of us have the strength of convincing speech; some of enthusiasm; some of creative potential. This card invites us to examine our strengths, and to work on them – by consciously digging them out and using them more. The other aspect of this card deals with invalidation. This is the minimalization (making something smaller or less significant) of what we believe in. We must never let others undermine us, either deliberately or unconsciously.

Negative Aspects

lazy • impulsive • showing off • aggressive • vanity • lust • uncontrolled sensuality

Key Words

vigilance • courage • loyalty • creativity • generosity • challenges • indulgence • proud/pride

Suggestions

- Put your knowledge into action.
- Develop your will.
- Link your head with your heart, and your heart with your will.

The Hermit

We find ourselves moving along a long trail
high into the mountains. We feel the cold,
biting winds tugging at our thin clothing. The air has become
thin too, and we have to breathe more deeply to try and stay
properly ventilated. It starts snowing and the light around us
begins to fade. It is nightfall and we are lost in these hills, far
from any shelter or sustenance. How distant seems any hope of
survival! From the distance, though, we see a light shining out
there in the dark. Could this be a light being carried by someone? Shall we venture forth against the blizzard to look? What –
or who – do we find? To what does he lead us?

The Hermit card teaches us about being separate from the material world. We all need to be alone from time to time. We need this space for growing, for nurturing, for being, for not 'doing' anything in particular.

A more problematic aspect of the Hermit card touches upon the feelings of alienation and isolation that so many people experience. The teaching of the Hermit is to show us that such times need not be bad experiences: being alone can give us the chance to look more deeply within and to review our life, our feelings and our emotions.

Negative Aspects

shy/introverted • alienation • isolation • unsociable • unable to relate to people • anxious

Key Words

spiritual journey • meditation/prayer • retreat • thinker • modest/humble • agile with words and hands • withdrawal

Suggestions

- Look for the goodness in people.
- Do voluntary work.
- Spend a couple of days alone in the woods.

The Wheel of Fortune

You stand before a great Wheel, which is slowly spinning. This Wheel reminds you of the changes in fortune which you yourself have gone through in your Journey up to this point. It reminds you of the good times and the difficult times you have been through. You visualize yourself on this wheel and can now feel more confident in dealing with any future problems you may encounter on the road ahead, knowing it will somehow work out. Similarly, you now know you will not be so elated when things work out well, as there will always be stormy periods that have to be gone through.

The Wheel of Fortune card raises many issues in our lives. What is our destiny? Can we change it? Or do we have to go through it all again in order to learn from it?

The principle of the Wheel is: nothing stays the same, we have to evolve all the time and move along with the flow. The Wheel of Fortune gives us not necessarily what we want, but what we need in order to progress.

Faith is another aspect of the Wheel. Faith is the ability to bounce back after you have had a setback. The Wheel also represents faith in the future. The Wheel reminds us that we have to think of tomorrow.

Negative Aspects

ups and downs • setback • overly optimistic • hiding behind destiny

Key Words

good fortune • abundance • opportunities in disguise • cycles • test of faith

Suggestions
- Appreciate your good fortune, and rejoice in the good fortune of others.
- Don't promise more than you can deliver.
- Develop your faith.

Justice

You find yourself in front of a huge set of scales. From beside you a figure appears, hooded, prodding you to step into one of the pans of the scales. You feel a sense of trepidation as you do so. Something – you are not sure what – has been placed in the other pan, which is now being counterbalanced against you. You feel the upward and downward motion of the pans as you swing to and fro. What will happen to you if the scales tip against you? Beside you, you can see strange shadowy forms, crouching in the darkness – they will set upon you if you should 'fail'. What happens next?

Justice stands for equilibrium. It represents the law of exchange: you take something and you must give something in return. If you can make both sides of the scale balance, it is justice.

We need to look at Justice not only in relation to material possessions, but also in relation to our feelings and thoughts. If we put too much emphasis on wealth and possessions, we are slowly diminishing the need to develop our spiritual life.

The Justice card teaches us about karma, which means that we will each be rewarded for the good we have done and punished for the bad.

Negative Aspects

injustice • indecision • unfairness • evil purpose • chaos • suffering • karmic debts

Key Words

balance • code of conduct • readjustment • legal matters • good judgement

Suggestions

- Report crime/oppose injustice.
- Be objective and fair in your views.
- Seek balance and equilibrium.

The Hanged Man

You are walking through a forest and come across a strange sight. Hanging upside down from a small scaffold is a man, with his arms tied behind his back. You see a small sign pinned to the side of the scaffold, which reads: 'This man is guilty of a crime. He is to hang here for one full day. If anyone cuts him down or brings him sustenance of any kind, they will receive the same punishment as him.' The man is clearly suffering. What do you do?

The Hanged Man card invites us to look at our hang-ups, our inhibitions which can hold us in fear and servitude. We don't have to be the victim.

Nothing much happens in the company of the Hanged Man. He just hangs around doing nothing, thus producing nothing. He stands for passivity. In fact, he is a bit like a weathercock. He constantly swings with the wind between comments, opinions. One minute he follows one belief and the next moment, another. His world is made of dreams. He likes to escape from it all. He is there to warn us against being similarly open to every influence.

This card asks us what we are prepared to sacrifice in order to be able to move on in life.

Negative Aspects

impressionable • resigned • victimized • unwilling to make decisions or take actions • seeing the world upside down

Key Words

obedient • visions • unselfish • vague • sacrifices • waiting • transition • delay • transcend

Suggestions

- Stop doing things to yourself if they are harmful.
- Don't be swayed by the winds of public opinion.
- Don't let your friends or relatives tell you what you should do or think.

Death

Gradually you become aware of yourself standing in a deep and very dark mist. You can't see far at all but, shivering against the cold, you start moving in a random direction to try to keep warm. Time passes by, and you seem no nearer to finding your way through this mist. Suddenly, standing right in your path, you see the silhouette of a human-like form, which seems to be waiting for you. You are a bit frightened at this, but decide to approach the figure to see if he can lead you to safety. As you draw closer, you see that the form carries a large scythe over his shoulder. What happens now?

Death is, in many ways, a commemoration of life! It is spring after a long and cold winter. When spring comes, there is a sense of renewal and freshness in the air. Animals, flora, fauna and human beings come to life again. Death is the symbol of rebirth.

The Death card shows us how very destructive it can be to hold on to things or people or harmful feelings. Thus, it encourages us to let go of those harmful habits and to set ourselves free again to start afresh. Ask yourself: What do you have to lose? Or what do you have to gain? Start now. Every end is a new beginning.

Negative Aspects

can't let go • afraid of change • misunderstood • obsessive • obstinate • vindictive

Key Words

resurrection • new directions • corrections • release • metamorphosed • tenacity • determined

Suggestions

• When you give up a bad habit, replace it with a good one.
• Don't be afraid to change.
• Learn to cut your losses and move on.

Temperance

You are walking along an open road, and you come across a flowing stream to one side, which gleams in a peculiar way. You stop to look at it more closely and, as you look at your own reflection, a rippling movement seems to cross your image in the water; you then see the reflection of someone else standing behind you. You turn around and there before you stands an angel, holding in each hand a jug, with water flowing in mid-air between them. The angel has come to give you a message. You struggle to speak, but cannot. Nonetheless, you seem able to communicate through your thoughts. What transpires between you and this angel?

The Temperance card refers to the process of being tested and of refinement. It gets us to look upon those experiences in life which have put us to the test and enabled us to become better people.

This card encourages us to develop our awareness of philosophy and religion. It also gets us to look at those things to which we give our support. If we are unhappy with something, we must remember we have the power to withdraw our support.

The Temperance card rules over healing and it teaches us about the many different kinds of alternative therapies that are now open to us.

Negative Aspects

stuck in the past • nothing wrong with me! • refusal to learn from past • traumas • too delicate

Key Words

new teaching • enlightenment • spiritual elevation • enhancing • fusion

Suggestions

- Cultivate your spirituality.
- Practice self-healing.
- Look into the past to understand the present.

The Devil

You stand in a dimly-lit hall. The air is chilly. You make your way down into a great hall which has no windows. You come to the foot of a grand staircase. On the walls to one side you see displayed various objects designed for punishment or penance: whips, branding irons, scourges, all intended to cause suffering through the sense of touch. Your foot slips on the blood that is splattered over the ground. Down the corridor someone screams in agony. What happens next?

The Devil represents all that is negative and seems to hold us back, or are we just blaming the wrong things for our own lack of determination and success? Are these barriers real or are they self-created to sabotage us?

The Devil card has much to do with lack of vision. People can get stuck in this card – as indeed they can in any other – only here it really is quite gloomy. This card gets us to confront our own negativity and suggests that we begin to look at ourselves more positively. We must love and accept ourselves and not sit in judgement and be self-condemnatory. The Devil card reminds us to keep hold of our ethical principles and not to compromise them, even if that means being ostracized by our peers.

Negative Aspects

ignorance • too much pride • revenge • greed • self-punishment • need to dominate • vices/sadism

Key Words

change of view • thinking • accepting/tolerance • future • respect • discipline • responsible

Suggestions

- When you are in doubt about your actions, look at your own motivations.
- Be gentle with yourself and others.
- Develop higher self-esteem.

The Tower

It is night, but lightning fills the sky, for a moment illuminating a volcano that is not completely dormant. A cold wind moves around you, that stirs anger and hostility, even if there is no cause. You can see a small building sitting on the slope of the volcano. It seems to have been there for ages, so old is its architecture. How has it survived the rumblings of the volcano? You begin to move closer to it and now can see that there is light coming from it and that the inhabitants are singing some kind of hymn, or liturgy. Activate this scenario.

The Tower is here to challenge the foundations of our lives. If the foundations upon which we build our lives are not solid, the thunderbolt of the Tower will destroy them completely. The effects of the Tower are quite devastating. They could manifest as a chain of disasters (you lose your keys, then your car gets stolen, then somebody breaks into your house, then you lose your job, etc), or as a nervous breakdown, an accident, an illness, etc.

Life on earth is a great school in which we are constantly put to the test. It is by passing through a series of trials that people gradually develop faith, hope and love. This card is here to teach us about courage in the face of adversity.

Negative Aspects

crumbling down • destructive • turmoil • building castles in the air • fury/violence • danger

Key Words

revelations • sudden tension • striking • agitation • warning/test

Suggestions
• Be willing to rebuild from scratch.
• Don't turn your energy inward.
• Build your life on stronger foundations.

The Star

You are out walking under a starry sky. The
dome of heaven all about you is filled with its
glorious gems, the stars and the Milky Way behind it. You stand
there in amazement, and you seem to grow in stature, becoming
taller, until you can almost reach out and touch the stars themselves.
Looking up to the Milky Way, you raise your arms and breathe
deeply from its downpouring radiance. To your side you see a
beautiful maiden, holding water vessels, one in each hand. You
cannot tell if she is human or angelic, but there is something
about her that is almost fairy-like. You speak out to her. What is
her answer?

The Star is the calm sea after the storm, as it represents tranquillity, serenity and peace of mind.

The Star card portrays a beautiful woman (the Goddess Nuit) pouring water from an urn to quench the thirst of humanity. This is the water of life that gives knowledge to all and knowledge gives life in return. Thus, the Star shows us how to nourish and water all that exists within and around so that it shall bear fruit.

The Star represents us as human beings getting together and sharing thoughts and knowledge to help one another. The Star touches upon the principle of humanitarianism in life.

Negative Aspects

disconnection • impersonal • lack of concern for humanitarian or environmental issues

Key Words

unselfish • dynamics of life • relationships • ideals • new possibilities • humanitarian

Suggestions
• Restore peace and love to your daily life.
• Support humanitarian organisations/be concerned with worldwide issues.
• Use your knowledge to create good for everyone.

The Moon

It is night, a sound of running water invites you to find out where it is coming from. You turn a corner and see a wide river, with twin towers standing beside it. You kneel down to drink from the side of the river and as you do so you hear the sound of distant thunder. As you look into the sky, you see a glorious full moon shining. Something in you now feels complete. What characters would you like to meet in this realm?

The Moon represents the subconscious, the realm of dreams, fears, memories, every kind of thinking not connected with the here and now. It contains the hopes and fears of the future and all the recollections of things that have already taken place.

The Moon card serves as a warning that all is not what it seems or looks. The Moon card also symbolizes reflection. The Moon is like a mirror, showing us a reflection of ourselves. It may not always be a pleasant picture. To look in that mirror may show us aspects of ourselves that we would rather not confront. Honesty is needed to shatter the illusions which we like to build up about ourselves.

Negative Aspects

touchy/moody • fears and phobias • psychosomatic illnesses • living in a dream land • overly sensitive

Key Words

dramatization • feeling not there • sensitivity • emanations • too imaginative • distorted reality

Suggestions
• Look to your dreams, keep a dream diary.
• Keep your feet firmly on the ground, don't be so strongly influenced by your emotions and imagination.
• Remember that most of your fears will never happen.

The Sun

You find yourself in a beautiful garden, full of
flowers of every description, colour and scent. You walk further
into the garden and at its centre you discover a fountain, from
which emerges a small rainbow cascade of water. You drink from
the cool water, noticing how cool it is in your hands and in your
mouth and throat. From behind you, you hear the sound of
children's voices. As you turn around you see two children,
both young, one boy and the other a girl. They could well be
twins. They take you by the hand and lead you further into the
garden. What happens to you this day?

The Sun illuminates our lives. If you know how to work with the Sun, the Sun will give you light (enlightenment), heat (warmth and love) and life (willpower to manifest).

The Sun card helps us see more clearly the reality of whatever we are dealing with. It is about objective truths, not just personal ones. This card is about action, construction, planning. Before embarking on any major project it is vital to construct a model of its workability before hand. We can't afford to just rush into anything on the basis that 'my intuition told me so'.

The Sun card also teaches us about the importance of physical exercise. What are you doing to take care of your body?

Negative Aspects

over-doing • burning one's fingers • waste of energy • over-extension

Key Words

open-hearted • happiness • alive • harmonious • ultimate love • creative • celebration • vacation

Suggestions
- Acknowledge the Sun's presence every day and thank him.
- Go for a walk in the park or the countryside if you want to know the Sun.
- May your thoughts be as luminous as the Sun.

Judgement

You find yourself walking through a desert scene.
There is no sound or movement here. The heat is unbearable.
You look up to the sky and see the dazzling sun in its canopy of
blue. You continue walking through the desert, the sand starts
running into the sides of your boots. As you move forward, you
can actually feel your body dehydrating. You start having
hallucinations about water – imagining rivers, streams, waves.
You continue further and feel the ground trembling beneath
your feet. As you look, cracks open in the earth's surface and
the ground starts gaping open. What happens now?

Judgement is about major changes, or transformation taking place in our lives. This card is concerned with how we judge others and even ourselves. When we are finally able to stop that, then we shall experience a powerful transformation in our lives.

This card is asking us to look at the major changes which our own lives have seen: can we see how we have changed as people through them? Have we mellowed and become better people, or worse?

This card is also about how we can change instead of skimming along the surface of problems and simply coping. So many people are reacting with their problems, illnesses, boyfriends, work, etc. instead of making the kind of changes that really need to take place.

Negative Aspects

manipulative • guilt/shame • fanatic • hard to quit • obsessions

Key Words

major change • turning point • resurrection • overcoming obstacles • self-discovery

Suggestions
• Be more adaptable.
• Change instead of coping.
• Go for a walk and explore what is around you.

The World

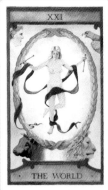

Before you stands a woman, naked, except for
a single length of purple silk, which is draped
across her shoulders. She dances before you and in her dancing
you see something incredibly symbolic of your own life and of
your Journey up to this point. But as you continue looking, you
see another symbol, that of the dance of the earth around the
sun and the beginning and end of all things. Everything seems
to be contained in the movements of this dancing girl. You find
yourself mesmerized. She invites you to join her in this dance,
she beckons you to get up out of your seat in the audience and
become her dancing partner. Join her!

The World is the last card of the Major Arcana and the fulfilment of each of them, if their lessons have been properly applied. The World represents success through your hard work. Not just in a materialistic sense, but more in the sense of having conquered all the barriers which have led up to this point.

The World card is about commitments and how we fulfil them. Have we fulfilled our commitments and if not, what are we going to do about them? This card also represents trust. Can you be trusted?

Excessive World card qualities result in people feeling that they must live their lives according to somebody else's expectations. They end up feeling they are carrying the weight of the World on their shoulders.

Negative Aspects

martyrdom • heavy burdens • lack of confidence • can't fulfil commitments

Key Words

worldly success • finality • achieving • realizing • accomplishment • wise

Suggestions

- Be responsible for yourself and others and the planet.
- Look at what you have achieved so far.
- Be thankful and grateful for your success.

The Minor Arcana

As outlined previously, the Minor Arcana consists of 56 cards which show everyday life situations, and the different kinds of people in the querent's life. The cards are divided into four suits: coins (or pentacles or discs), cups, swords and wands.

This section of the Tarot gives us a great deal of guidance on how we can be more effective and empower ourselves so that we can in turn empower others.

The suit of Coins, Pentacles or Discs

This suit represents the element Earth. It stands for material and financial conditions.

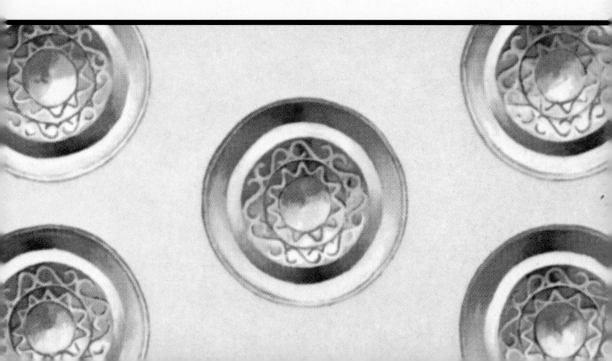

Ace of Coins

The Ace of Coins represents the purest form of the element of Earth. It stands for opportunities that spring up from the physical universe. It deals with reality and practicality.

This card transforms your skills or talents into assets. It is through this card that we can benefit financially or materially from what we know and can do.

Negative Aspects
out of touch with the physical universe

Key Words
beneficial • profitable • satisfaction • resources • stability • foundation

Two of Coins

This card represents movement from one financial or material condition to the next. It shows us that we need to become more adaptable or flexible in what we do. That way, we can easily develop different skills, or relocate and work somewhere else, without any trouble or difficulty.

Negative Aspects
rigidity • dislike of change • stuck in a rut

Key Words
versatility • transition • change • different circumstances or places

Three of Coins

This card encourages us to learn practical and useful skills. It could be on the work side or in other areas of life. Many years ago, people knew how to build houses, or make clothing, or how to hunt in order to survive. This card urges us to regain those fundamental life skills.

Negative Aspects
relying on others to do it all • not interested in learning

Key Words
self-sufficiency • learning the basics • never too late • being practical

Four of Coins

This card represents power on the material level. It is concerned with one's own security – financial or material. When we have a regular source of income, or we have saved money, we can relax and enjoy life. What we have accumulated will be sufficient for us to feel safe. How can you make yourself more secure?

Negative Aspects
physical or material self-gratification • greed • resources lying dormant

Key Words
consolidation • saving • conservative • possession • protection

Five of Coins

This card represents unexpected or unforeseen financial or material loss, possibly resulting from unemployment. It encourages us to develop new skills or abilities to help us find a job, or earn a living. Also in this card there is a feeling of neediness. We need to be needed. We have to change this equation in order to progress. Look after you.

Negative Aspects
poverty • putting blame on others or circumstances • lack of self worth

Key Words
necessity • weakness • social limitation

Six of Coins

This card represents the law of commerce, thus exchanges. The lesson of this card is to work in a mutual exchange with people. Don't disadvantage yourself just to please others. Value your work, or a skill you have, and ask for something in return.

Negative Aspects
overspending • wasting time and effort • giving to the undeserving

Key Words
trade • balancing • business strategy • transaction • speculation

Seven of Coins

This card represents the harvest time springing up from the fruits of our labour. If we make an effort, and we are willing to work hard, we shall reap the rewards of our work. It encourages us to keep ourselves busy and productive, and to cultivate our skills and abilities.

Negative Aspects
workaholic • laziness • harvesting somebody else's hard work • expecting miracles

Key Words
reliable • realization • patience • perseverance • growth

Eight of Coins

This card represents craftsmanship. Craftsmanship is simply the mastery of one's skills through self-discipline, dedication and determination. In order to be good at what we want to do, we must practice. Practice makes perfect.

Negative Aspects
too perfectionist • too demanding on oneself • not practising

Key Words
apprentice • specialization • in demand • meticulous • manual skills • the arts

Nine of Coins

This card represents recognition in the eyes of others. In this card, we have been acknowledged for our work. We feel satisfied because we have gained material status and esteem from our peers. Thus, this card represents achievement on the material level. Have people ever noticed your work and effort?

Negative Aspects
showing off • put on pedestal • ego in the way of doing • obsessed with appearance

Key Words
fame • rank • success • promotion prize • increase

Ten of Coins

This card represents joint financial decisions or major investments. In many ways, this card shows the importance of 'family' or communal business. Thus, this card represents us sharing what we know with other people in order to profit together.

Negative Aspects
profit not shared • not viable • big income for bosses but low pay for workers

Key Words
corporation • deals • financial commitment • employers

Page of Coins

This card represents someone who is looking for a new direction in life or new responsibilities. What do you want to achieve at the end of the day? Would you like to be in the same situation for years or would you like to have more control over your life? That is why we must look ahead in order to plan for the future.

Negative Aspects
lack of concern • no control over one's profession • missing opportunities to progress

Key Words
first job • new horizons • doing something completely different • improvement

Knight of Coins

This card represents a man who is keen to develop the work aspect of his life. That is why this man wants to develop his skills and abilities in order to progress. He has something to look forward to in his life and work. Do you have objectives too?

Negative Aspects
lost his sense of direction • unemployed • bored with work/can't find his vocation

Key Words
well-prepared • persistent • planning • ambition • professional

Queen of Coins

This card represents a woman who is keen to develop the work side of her life. She wants to be involved in the financial or material aspects. She likes the good things in life.

Care, precision and frugality are her hallmarks. Under her influence, 'customer satisfaction' and a high level of service are guaranteed.

Negative Aspects
lost sense of direction • confused • bored with life

Key Words
independent financially • practical with money • knows how to budget

King of Coins

This card represents someone at the top of whatever they are doing. In this card, we see achievement through one's own effort and talents. This person is also very encouraging and supportive towards others. This card encourages us to flourish and prosper.

Negative Aspects
dull • working with figures • talks business all the time

Key Words
steady • permanent • prodigal • calculated • administrative

The suit of Cups

This suit is linked with the element of Water. It represents the subjective world of inner experiences, such as feelings, emotions and sensations.

Ace of Cups

The Ace of Cups represents the higher qualities of love and of joy. We feel flooded with gratitude towards all the beauty which surrounds us. Our souls overflow with love. Our feelings are as pure as the water from mountain springs! Love has finally ripened.

Negative Aspects
on an artificial high • emptiness • not fully happy • impurity

Key Words
contentment • abundance • joy • kindness • birth • peace • fullness

Two of Cups

This card represents a new relationship, or a new stage (beginning) within an existing relationship. In this card, we have the mutual exchange of feelings and emotions. We are willing to share our experiences and should be open to new friendships or relationships. How close are your relationships?

Negative Aspects
locked in a relationship • don't want to know • can't receive from

Key Words
new friendships • contacts • renewal • love • harmony • affinity

Three of Cups

This card represents reunion or getting together with old friends or relatives. It shows how we can reciprocate feelings of love or friendship to each other. There is a feeling of celebration, of joyfulness. We feel loved, therefore we love in return.

Negative Aspects
can't feel love • not enjoying people's company • avoiding old friends

Key Words
eating • drinking • marriage • meeting old friends

Four of Cups

This card represents reaching out for new friendships or relationships. It usually talks about things we take for granted. We are looking for someone or something, and when it finally comes into our life, we just can't be bothered. What is stopping you from reaching out?

Negative Aspects
holding back • waiting for things to happen without effort • withdrawal

Key Words
taking what is on offer • making the first move • opportunities to meet people

Five of Cups

This card represents dependency on others. It shows how we tend to cling too much to people's promises or words. It also shows disappointment which results from the failure of reality to match expectations. This is why this card encourages us to look ahead, instead of depending on other people or lamenting their broken promises.

Negative Aspects
disillusionment • sadness •
disappointment • living in the past

Key Words
relying too heavily on other people •
caring • being more rational

Six of Cups

This card represents learning to give and receive emotionally. It shows us how we can develop our relationships into a long-lasting friendship or love affair. With this card, we are full of good intentions for each other. We feel like children again. There is a sense of harmony. Are you able to get in touch with your 'child within'?

Negative Aspects
giving without receiving and vice
versa • expecting something in return

Key Words
friendship • socializing • affinity •
growing relationship

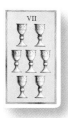

Seven of Cups

This card represents emotional confusion. What are your priorities in life? You might want to be rich, or be a farmer, or look like Marilyn Monroe. Whatever you want to be, you have to sort out what comes first in your life. We must come down from our comforting clouds in order to realize our dreams.

Negative Aspects
daydreams • escapism • fantasies • make-believe

Key Words
being realistic • using dreams constructively

Eight of Cups

This card represents our quest for a deeper meaning in life. Where is our life taking us? We must each find our own individual destiny. What is the purpose of life? What do we have to realize? This card shows us the way. The answer is within us.

Negative Aspects
looking for a substitute • puzzle • superficiality • denying deep emotional needs

Key Words
reflection • pondering • searching • understanding • depth

Nine of Cups

This card represents experiencing life as a celebration. We must enjoy life and celebrate it. Let's not forget that no matter how bad things are – or have been – we are still better off then many people on this planet. We must learn to look on the bright side.

Negative Aspects
being happy but only on the surface • too many parties • excessive eating or drinking

Key Words
parties • eating and drinking • earthly pleasure • good things in life

Ten of Cups

This card represents an emotional commitment. It shows a union or communion with others or oneself. We have to be committed in anything we feel or do in order to get involved in our life. When we commit ourselves, we feel at one with the universe.

Negative Aspects
unstable • don't want to get involved

Key Words
marriage • dedication • unity

Page of Cups

This card represents new social or professional contacts. In order to grow emotionally, we must start to meet new people. And then we can learn about ourselves, and how to build new affinities. This card is inviting us to give new people a chance to enter our lives.

Negative Aspects
too introverted • feeling insecure • naïve • withdrawn • shy

Key Words
learning about oneself through others • romance

Knight of Cups

This card represents sensitivity or receptivity in a man. In this card, a man is looking for a meaningful relationship.
The Knight brings out those feelings which involve taking the initiative. When we feel those emotional needs banging on the door of our mind, we should go with them. Who knows where they might lead us?

Negative Aspects
can't express himself emotionally • too impressionable • sentimental

Key Words
flirty • dreamy • artistic

Queen of Cups

This card symbolizes sensitivity or receptivity in a woman. She represents the receptive side of our emotional nature, i.e. our individual ability to enjoy all the different emotions or feelings which are brought out by someone entering or staying in our lives.

Negative Aspects
easily impressionable • taking for granted • insensitive to people's needs • sentimental

Key Words
artistic • mother figure • caring • stable

King of Cups

This card represents an emotional mature man. The King symbolizes a kind of emotional coming of age, for either a man or a woman. For example, no longer do we need to get upset if someone we find attractive doesn't want to know. We now have the ability to move on without attachment.

Negative Aspects
dull • pleasing others • between two seas • too sugary

Key Words
stable • eccentric • creative • father figure

The suit of Swords

This suit represents the element of Air. It symbolizes states of mind, and states of conflict.

Ace of Swords

The Ace of Swords represents the purest form of the element of Air. It indicates a breakthrough of some kind on the mental level. This card distinguishes, separates and arranges, so as to clarify where we stand.

Negative Aspects
self-limiting thought • difficulty in communicating • can't concentrate • over-analytical

Key Words
determination • intelligence • clear-headed • victory

Two of Swords

This card represents indecision. What should we do? Here we have the conflict between mind (thought) and heart (feeling). This card shows us how we can balance both mind and heart. Are your mind and heart in conflict when it comes to making a decision?

Negative Aspects
ignoring feelings • don't want to see

Key Words
see both sides • crossroads • balance • turning point

Three of Swords

This card represents heartbreak unless one can communicate better. If we have been hurt badly we must communicate what is in our heart. It is difficult for each of us to truly open up in this way. But only when we get it all off our chest – the hurt, rejection, humiliation and loss – can we start afresh.

Negative Aspects
hiding • pain in the heart • upset

Key Words
personal • using words to express pain

Four of Swords

This card represents worries and tensions. Here we have to relax more in order to let go of all negative thoughts. Take time to go for walks in the park to empty your mind. Take some time off to relax. Learn to breathe properly; breathing helps to slow down the brain waves.

Negative Aspects
stress • tired • anxious

Key Words
release • calm • slow down

Five of Swords

This card represents the parting of ways. Here we have the end of a battle, we feel defeated.

This card encourages us to be careful of unnecessary quarrels. The loss will be ours. Do you start to quarrel when you know you have nothing to fall back on?

Negative Aspects
separation • rejection • deceit • shame • pessimistic • lies

Key Words
troublesome • retreat • casualties

Six of Swords

This card represents moving away from negativity. It shows how to overcome difficulties by finding new ideas and solutions.

This card also shows withdrawal – retreat. Sometimes we have to pull out of a situation in order to deal with it. There is no shame in this, if that is what seems best for us at the time.

Negative Aspects
static thinking • not searching

Key Words
thinking through • brainstorming • spontaneous thinking • suggestion

Seven of Swords

This card represents sacrifices. One has to give up something good for something better in order to progress in life.

Another aspect of this card is being 'ripped off'. To protect what is ours we do have to exercise vigilance – we have to be aware of what is going on and of the possible consequences of being too open.

Negative Aspects
coward • not willing to let go of our self-limiting thoughts • ripping off

Key Words
progress • sorting out • stealth

Eight of Swords

This card represents frustration. Here we can learn to be a bit more patient.

This card also epitomizes restrictions we are imposing willingly or unwillingly upon ourselves. Because we remain blindfolded, we are not really seeing what the real problems are, or where they are coming from.

Negative Aspects
bondage • victim • impatient • disconnection • stress

Key Words
can't escape • finding • waiting • trapped

Nine of Swords

This card represents isolation. Here we have to learn to open up new lines or channels of communication. We must talk about what is holding us back. It seems in this card that we must go through a confessional in order to set ourselves free from the prison we have created. What is holding you back?

Negative Aspects
guilt • things we have done wrong • depression • repression • hands are tied

Key Words
recognize • admit • reveal • truth • isolation

Ten of Swords

In this card, we have to acknowledge the end of an era in order to begin another one. Here, we experience pain and/or suffering, and there is nothing we can do to stop it. Instead of dwelling on loss and pain we must learn to forgive and let go. Major changes are coming, go along with them to turn them to your advantage.

Negative Aspects
revenge • mental anguish • disgust

Key Words
result • out of one's system

Page of Swords

This card represents eagerness to rush into battles or conflicts. Here we have someone quite inexperienced in dealing with his own ego. This card encourages us not to rush into conflict or to fight other people's fights. Because, at the end of the day, it is you who is going to get hurt!

Negative Aspects
don't start something you can't stop • unprotected

Key Words
willing to take a stand • insecure • not knowing all the facts and figures

Knight of Swords

This card represents power by manipulation or force. When it refers to ourselves, we have to learn to be more tactful or diplomatic. When this card shows someone else or another influence in our lives, it is a warning for us not to hand over our rights too easily.

Negative Aspects
aggressive with words • stroppy • angry • impetuous • invalidation

Key Words
balance of power • gentleness

Queen of Swords

This card represents a determined woman who has erected barriers between herself and others. This woman is very difficult to approach, she stands strongly in her position. This card can show the kind of woman who knows what she wants, and isn't inhibited about going after it.

Negative Aspects
critical • stubborn • questioning • suspicious • revengeful • cold

Key Words
be open • don't be negative • maintaining your barriers • keeping your own space

King of Swords

This card represents someone who has won the war, and now has to establish the peace.

In this card we have someone of authority who is on guard all the time. We must allow people to express themselves instead of judging them non-stop. You can establish your own authority by allowing others to occupy centre stage more.

Negative Aspects
military • bitter • prejudicial • intolerant • headstrong

Key Words
enjoying life • be open minded • allow mistakes

The suit of Wands

This suit represents the element of Fire. It symbolises energy, action and will-power.

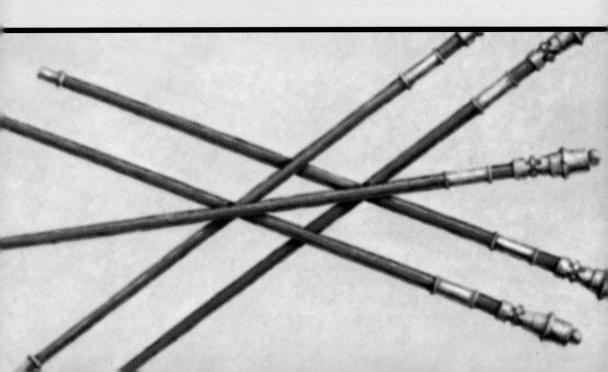

Ace of Wands

The Ace of Wands represents the purest form of the element of Fire. This card emphasizes energy and action. It stands for new initiative or enterprise which has been activated. Individuality is brought forth and emphasized, not compromised.

Negative Aspects
lack of initiative • lack of energy

Key Words
action • vitality • consume • dynamic • will-power • truth • creativity

Two of Wands

This card represents the giving and receiving of good advice. It encourages us to exchange our ideas and to put them into motion. We need that outflow of energy to see if what we have to offer is workable.

Negative Aspects
ask for help, but don't listen when it's given • wait for people to start off ideas • can't make decisions

Key Words
starting off new ideas • listening to people's point of view

Three of Wands

This card represents leading the way by your own example. Here we have to initiate what we want to create. If we preach something that we are not doing, people will not follow us.
In this card, we find the principle of leadership. Are you a leader, i.e. do you show the way for others?

Negative Aspects
talking but not doing • lack of will

Key Words
operative • inspiration • dominion • demonstrating • purposeful • honest

Four of Wands

This card represents participating with others toward a common goal. In this card, we learn how to help and support each other. We learn about teamwork and co-operative work. It emphasizes being able to harmonize with others so that more than just our own personal objectives can be attained.

Negative Aspects
feel useless • can't belong

Key Words
dynamics of life • completion • building a better world

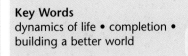

Five of Wands

This card represents fierce competition. We need to push forward with determination in order to get our point or idea across.

This card represents challenges. We each of us at times must fight hard for what we want. Are you competitive enough?

Negative Aspects
friction • too aggressive • over imposing • hasty

Key Words
argumentative • courage • drive • games • sport • strive

Six of Wands

This card represents victory. Here, we have accomplished our task, and we feel admired by others.

Each of us has accomplished something – having a child, showing bravery in the face of adversity. So we're not all rich or famous. But there are many kinds of achievement, and who is to say which kind is superior to any other?

Negative Aspects
too vain • pomposity • pretence

Key Words
winning • confidence • achievement • self-esteem • impressive

Seven of Wands

This card represents having to tackle your problems one at a time before they overwhelm you. Do you confront or run away from your problems? Instead, why not write them down, in order of their magnitude. Now try and work out how you could resolve each issue in a practical way.

Negative Aspects
overtaken • ignoring issues • erratic • overwhelming

Key Words
effort • obstacles • courage • handle

Eight of Wands

This card represents the principle of life speeding up. Here we are very busy, there are lots of activities and much movement. When we 'get on a roll', new ideas and projects open before us. The mother of all action is enthusiasm, so we have to stay positive. We also have to be aware of the practical steps we must take in order to turn our projects into reality.

Negative Aspects
too busy • travelling too much • all over the place • don't have time • restless

Key Words
action • very creative • many ideas • working on different projects

Nine of Wands

This card represents breaking barriers. Here we have to learn to trust others or to delegate. We can't do it on our own, we have to allow people to give us a hand. By allowing others to give, you will also be making them feel more positive about their lives as well.

Negative Aspects	Key Words
don't need anyone • pride • refusing support • feel weak	generate trust • show people

Ten of Wands

This card represents burdens. Here we are taking on board more than we can handle. We have allowed people to overburden us with their responsibilities or problems.

There are times when it is worthwhile to carry such a burden: the long-term benefit may be considerable. But just plodding along in this way without any destination in sight is not.

Negative Aspects	Key Words
feeling obliged to carry burdens • trying to help too much	devotion • obligation • don't get involved • pressure

Page of Wands

This card represents learning or travelling. Here we are approaching life philosophically. On this road, we have much to learn about the spiritual aspect of life.

In this card, we are open-minded to new adventures, new people, new ideas, new possibilities. This card is about confronting our limitations, and then expanding them.

Negative Aspects
wrong intention • too much effort • refusal to learn

Key Words
games • truth • reason • human study

Knight of Wands

This card represents a dynamic male energy. The Knight portrays the quality of being enthusiastic. He is forceful, extrovert and full of life.

He is an inspirational force which gives us a vision of how things might be better. He incites to action, to get moving!

Negative Aspects
macho • over imposing • passionate • impulsive

Key Words
vigilant • lively • impatient • aggressive • optimism • exploration

Queen of Wands

This card portrays an independent minded woman. She stands on her own two feet. She is strong and supportive. She is not going to wait around for things to happen to her; she will make them happen herself! She will instigate her own relationships, and if they don't work out, she will go it alone.

Negative Aspects
too bossy • obstinate

Key Words
friendly • active • initiator •
attractive • warmth • helping • guide

King of Wands

This card represents a man of leadership and inspiration. He is a teacher figure. He guides, controls and directs. Under his influence, some semblance of order is achieved – he encourages us to reach our full potential, he pushes us to our limits. He protects us, but expects our support in his battles as well.

Negative Aspects
too domineering • dictatorial • rude

Key Words
force • power of command •
responsible • management

Using the Cards

Getting started

How to select a deck

It is important to select a deck that is right for you. There are many decks on the market these days, so you may well wonder where to begin.

It is important to avoid anything that is too specialised. There are many 'cultural' Tarot decks, based around Native Americans, wild animals, herbs or specific themes, such as the Celts, Arthurian legend, and the Vikings. Once you have a good grasp of the symbolism of the Tarot, you can move on and deal with the specific imagery of any such deck.

You should have a good look around, and select a deck that seems 'right' for you. Make sure that the deck has pictures for the Minor Arcana cards, as well as those in the Major Arcana; otherwise it will mean a major block to learning their meanings, and you will be forced to rely on a massive amount of memorisation. In those decks where every card bears a picture, you can easily see what is going on and start linking the cards together.

Another point is that you should definitely throw away the little booklets which accompany each new Tarot deck. They are sometimes written in a very negative light which only puts the recipient 'at effect', rather than empowering them to become more 'at cause' over life.

A good deck to start with would be the Rider Waite or Morgan Greer. If you already have a working knowledge of the Tarot, then you may well like to get my Dragon Tarot deck, and see what this has to offer you.

Opening the deck

When you open the deck, do it in a respectful way. You could light a candle, and let opening the pack be a 'consecrated' act. Some people like to rub a little essential oil into their new cards. Whatever method you choose, try to let your entry into the domain of the Tarot be a special experience.

Make friends with all the inhabitants of your deck – you will be getting to know each and every one of them very well indeed; they will be guiding you on the adventure ahead into this realm of new discovery!

Reading the cards

You can either read the cards for yourself, or for others. It is difficult
though to be objective when laying out the cards for yourself, as you
might want to hear a particular message and be unreceptive to other
aspects of advice and guidance which the Tarot can offer. In laying the
cards out for a friend, or someone who has asked you for a consultation,
it is best if they are present with you, although it is possible to do
readings for someone at a distance.

Shuffling and laying out the cards

First, the cards are shuffled. If you are
consulting the cards for yourself, stop the
shuffling when you feel that the moment is
'right'. If someone else is shuffling, let them
go on until they feel that they have shuffled
enough. Only a few minutes will normally
suffice; don't let them shuffle for much
longer than that. If you are reading the
cards for someone at a distance who wants
a reading, e.g. over the telephone, ask them
to tell you when to stop. Here, you are
doing the mechanics of the actual shuffling,
while it is they who stop the process; there
is a synchronicity involved in determining
which cards will come up in a reading.

 Now, lay out the cards. There is no 'one
way', or even 'best way' of doing this.
The cards, however, are usually laid down in
specific patterns, or what are known as
'spreads'. The spreads on pages 105–116 are
suggestions, but ones which I think you will
get a lot out of if you try them.

Interpreting the spread

It is not possible to give the meanings of the cards as if they were frozen in stone, carved definitively for all time, for all people, and in all situations. An individual card will shift in its meaning for the querent; at one point in their life it will refer more to one thing than another. It will reflect back what they need to know, depending on where they are in their Journey at the moment of seeking reference.

In working your way through a spread in a reading, go systematically at first, until you get the feel of how it all fits together. Remember that there may be inconsistencies in what seems to be showing in the spread; on the one hand this may well be because people's lives are riddled with inconsistencies and contradictions. On the other hand, you will have to learn how to 'fine tune' your readings to make it all fit together.

Be intuitive, and don't try to apply the meaning of each card literally, or 'by the book'. Try to get a more 'general' feeling of each card, and let that sense guide you through the spread. Remember also that the art of Tarot readership might take a bit of time to perfect; so don't let any hidden standard which you might feel you have to live up to make you feel overly critical about your achievements!

Above all, keep the reading simple!

Tips on Tarot reading for others

The main categories which you will be expected to cover in a reading are:

1. Money: investments, savings, gambles
2. Ambitions: potentials, secret desires, ambitions
3. Career: job change/title change, advancement, conflicts within workplace
4. Love life/sex life: remember that these two are rarely the same
5. Expectations: dreams, fantasies, predictions
6. Health: positive as well as negative influences
7. Travel: short and long journeys, people returning from the past, business trips, tourism.

To read the cards for someone else is a big responsibility. You must be careful what you say to others, and aware of the possible implications of your reading.

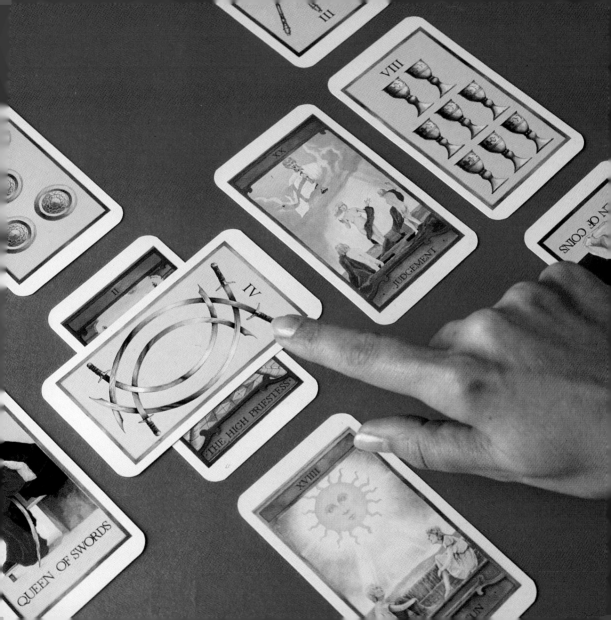

1 Allow the querent to ask questions. By answering their questions you can more effectively personalise the reading.

2 Avoid negative predictions. Someone who is troubled by worries or has had disappointment in their life needs a boost to their self-esteem, a greater belief in themselves.

3 Agree with your querent's views. Most people actually know the answers to their problems. They merely need some emotional support.

4 Advise your querent in a common-sense way. Most people are interested in practical alternatives to their problems.

5 You can feel free to move between past, present and future as you go through the cards.

6 Be authentic – don't be trapped into making things up just for the sake of having something to say.

7 Do be careful of predictions regarding health and legal matters. These things are best left in the hands of professionals.

8 Blend your statements into a story format. Don't give the impression that you are delivering a staccato-like string of isolated statements.

9 Create a comfortable atmosphere where you are doing the reading.

10 Constantly plant positive seeds – most predictions become self-fulfilling. The querent will make it come out that way.

11 Clarify predictions: be specific if you can. You can be guided by the questions you are asked, allowing your answers to become increasingly specific.

12 Channel intuitive information to your querent as part of the reading. Don't be afraid of being intuitive.

About reversed cards

By reversed cards we mean cards that come out upside down when you lay them out. Some people attach more significance to this than others. There are no rigid rules, but basically a reversed card might mean delay, a mitigation, an insufficient or conversely an excessive quality to the meaning of the card. It just puts more of a question mark over the meaning of that particular card, but don't get stumped by it!

It is possible to get very mechanistic and dogmatic in interpreting the cards. Reading the cards isn't really like this. You have to keep in view the person's life, and make sure that the cards fit into it, and not the other way round. When you start using your intuitive

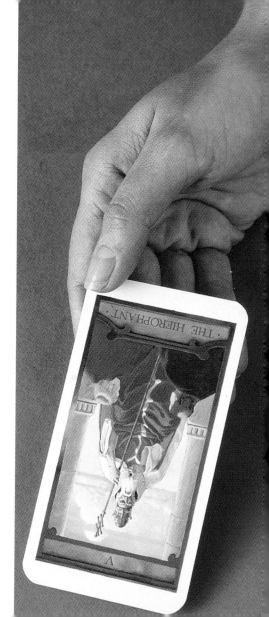

aspect you will be able to set aside the exact meanings of the cards and go by feelings as well.

So even if a card is reversed, don't immediately jump to the 'opposite' meaning. For example, if you have the Three of Swords reversed, it doesn't mean that the querent is heartbroken. It would probably mean that he/she has suppressed a lot of feelings, and that these will need a lot of help in being released.

Timing

Some Tarot readers have tried to find a way of determining the time when such and such will happen. This is, in my experience, very difficult. What we are looking at in the Tarot is a person's karma. There is no system of using cards to determine when something might occur.

You may get an intuitive flash, but you may not. Don't get pressurised into putting a time limit on something which you know in your heart is not likely. Sometimes the pressure from a querent can be quite considerable, which is understandable when you think about how frustrating it must be to be told something but not to have an 'expected time of arrival' given as well.

Spreads

So far we have looked at the individual meanings of the cards, and how they can be used to empower us in different ways. Now we shall look at how the cards are set out in various patterns, and what the combined message of a set of cards might be. Here are a variety of spreads for you to choose from.

The Crossroads Spread

This is an excellent spread to use in a dilemma – when you are at a crossroads in your life. If you have two specific courses of action open to you, you should consult this spread.

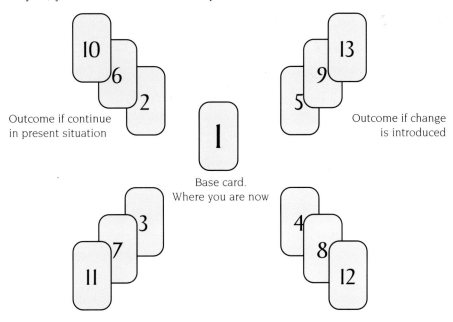

Outcome if continue
in present situation

Base card.
Where you are now

Outcome if change
is introduced

Influences of the recent past

Long term karmic influence

The Triadic Spread

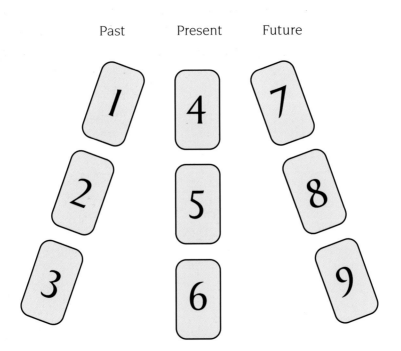

Past   Present   Future

This is a very simple spread, in which the cards you lay out on the left will represent the past, those in the middle the present, and those on the right the future. You can lay out as many cards as you like on either stack, and elucidate as far as you wish, but it is best to keep it to three in each stack, at least until you get the hang of it. This symbol was used by the ancient Druids, and shows the rays of the sun descending to earth. Thus it is a symbol of teaching, and enlightenment.

The Astrological Spread

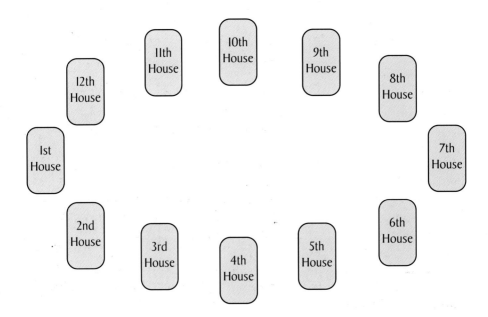

1st House (Aries and Mars) Basic personality: psychological motivation, personal qualities, disposition and temperament.

2nd House (Taurus and Venus) Possessions: work, personal worth, values. Attitudes towards security, possessions and partners.

3rd House (Gemini and Mercury) Communication: brothers, sisters, relatives, early education, environment, transport.

4th House (Cancer and the Moon) Domestic life: home, mother.

5th House (Leo and the Sun) Love life: creativity, pleasure, children, love affairs, amusement.

6th House (Virgo and Mercury) Work life: routine work, health, diet exercise, hobbies.

7th House (Libra and Venus) One to one relationships: partnerships, marriage, contracts.

8th House (Scorpio and Pluto) Major changes: sex, inheritance, investment, other people's resources.

9th House (Sagittarius and Jupiter) Learning: higher education, long-distance travel, ideals, dreams, challenge, beliefs, philosophy.

10th House (Capricorn and Saturn) Achievements: aspirations, ambitions, careers, father.

11th House (Aquarius and Uranus) Social life: objectives, friends.

12th House (Pisces and Neptune) Mystical life: seclusion, escapism, faith, institutions.

This spread works on the basis of the 12 astrological houses, although you do not need any prior knowledge of astrology in order to use it. The cards should be placed in an anti-clockwise direction, from the 1st House to the 12th House.

The Tree of Life Spread

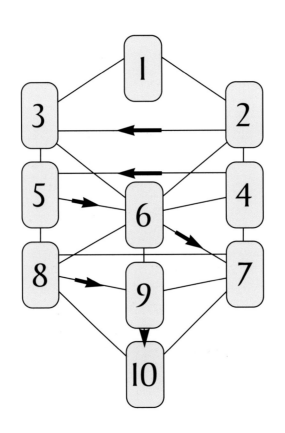

1. Neptune: Individual relationship with infinity/spirit/god.

2. Uranus: Revolutionary change, influence, inventiveness.

3. Saturn: Sense of limitation, lessons, disciplines, responsibilities.

4. Jupiter: Area in which blessings manifest, optimism, positivity.

5. Mars: Area of combat, personal battles.

6. Sun: Personal development, growth through life.

7. Venus: Creative, artistic area, harmony, accord.

8. Mercury: Communication, how one is learning, studying.

9. Moon: Intuition, psychic abilities.

10. Earth: Physical universe, real and tangible experiences.

Here you lay out the cards in the pattern shown. Each card epitomizes the influence of one of the Spheres of the Tree, which represents an area of your life and the work confronting you in it. This spread is deeply mystical, is ideal for looking at your own life, and should be consulted rarely. Some say it should only be done once in your life.

The Relationship Spread

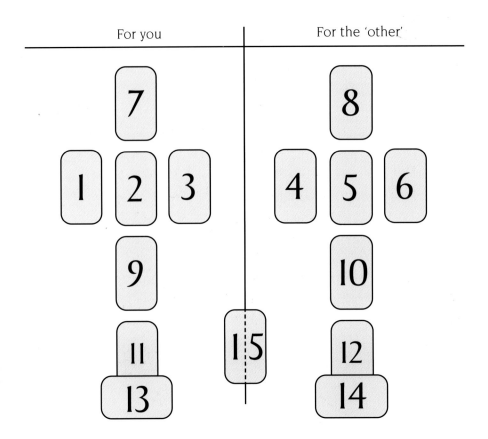

For you | For the 'other'

7   8

1   2   3   4   5   6

9   10

11   15   12

13   14

This spread is great for looking at any relationship – but especially where you and the other person are connected with love and/or desire.

1   What you are bringing into the relationship.
2   Where you are now, in relation to the other person.
3   What you are hoping to get from the relationship.
4   What the other person is bringing into their relationship with you.
5   What they are getting out of it.
6   What they are hoping to achieve/experience with you.
7   How you see the other person.
8   How they see you.
9   How you saw him/her when you first met.
10   How the other person saw you on your first meeting.
11   Your own anxieties/unconscious fears.
12   The other person's anxieties/unconscious fears.
13   External influences upon you.
14   External influences upon the other person.
15   Where the relationship will go.

The Celtic Cross

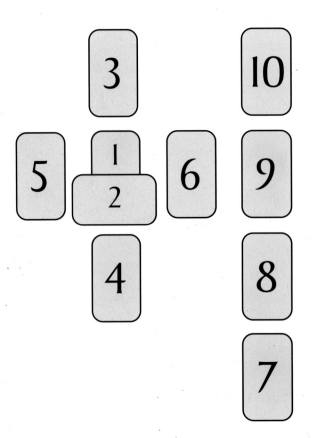

1   The general situation.
2   The general situation in more detail.
3   On the person's mind.
4   The influences of the last three years.
5   The influences of the last year.
6   The influences of the coming year.
7   Doorway from the present to the future.
8   Personal life.
9   Hopes or anxieties.
10   The overview – the 'by the way'.

This spread is good for looking at someone else's life, although it is not quite so useful for looking at your own.

   The first two cards show different aspects of the present situation. The third card shows us what is on the querent's mind. The fourth gives us an idea of what the influence of the last three years or so has been. It is also the 'base' of the cross, where it rests upon the ground, and therefore what is the actual foundation of the querent's situation. The fifth card shows us the last six months to one year, although it can show even more recent influences than that. The sixth card shows us the influences of the year ahead, while the seventh represents the doorway from the present into the future – in other words, how the querent moves from his present situation into the future influences. Whereas the sixth card tends to show what will be happening to the querent from external sources, this card shows what he needs to do in order to maximise the benefits he will receive from them. The eighth card gives an insight into the querent's personal life, and the ninth represents his or her hopes or anxieties. The tenth card provides us with an overview, as well as raising some issues not addressed in cards one to nine. The first nine cards hang together, while the tenth is really the beginning of a new chain of interpretation.

In order to 'open up' this spread, you can either get the querent to pick out additional cards or just deal them straight off the top of the stack over the relevant card in the basic spread, taking the symbolism to relate to the area for which you require greater elucidation. You can use this enhancing technique either to answer specific questions, or because you require more information than the basic ten cards are coming up with.

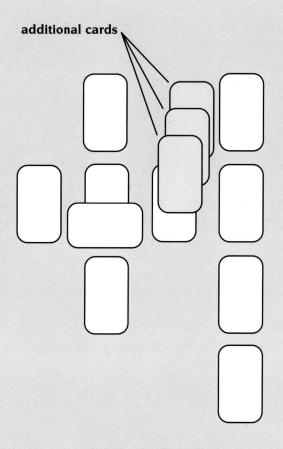

additional cards

Enhancing Technique

Where To Go From Here

The Tarot will be your really close companion on the trail that lies ahead. The insights which it gives you will always be useful, and we would encourage you to continue with your work. The more you help others, the more your own life will open up; the more you develop yourself, the more useful you will be to those around you.

You don't have to read a pile of books in order to understand something. You may want to read around the subject, though, and see what other people are saying about it. Feel free, by all means, but never let somebody else's theory become a substitute for your own realisation and wisdom.

The best way of continuing to develop is through helping others to do the same, so when you come across someone who is interested in finding out about the Tarot, talk about your own experiences and share your knowledge. By meeting others, you will also have the opportunity to share their insights as well.

Useful Addresses

UNITED KINGDOM

Festival for Mind, Body and Spirit
New Life Promotions
Arnica House
170 Campden Hill Road
London W8 7AS
Telephone: 020 7938 3788
Fax: 020 7723 7256

Mysteries
9/11 Monmouth Street
Covent Garden
London WC2H 9DA
Telephone: 020 7240 3688
For tarot decks, books, supplies, also tarot courses and readings.

Thorsons
HarperCollins*Publishers*
77-85 Fulham Palace Road
Hammersmith
London W6 8JB
Telephone: 020 8741 7070
Fax: 020 8307 4440
Thorsons publish a very wide range of tarot decks and books.
Free catalogue on request.

Watkins Bookshop
21 Cecil Court
Leicester Square
London WC2N 4EZ
Telephone: 020 7836 2182
Fax: 020 7836 6700
Has a very wide and famous selection of second-hand and hard to find books on the tarot, and other related mystical subjects.

David Westnedge Co.
5 Ferrier Street
London SW18 1SN
Telephone: 020 8871 2654
Fax: 020 8877 1241
For tarot decks and books.

USA

U.S. Games Systems Inc.
179 Ludlow Street
Stamford
CT 06902, USA
Telephone: (001) 203 353 8400
Fax: (001) 203 353 8431
For tarot decks, supplies and books.

Taraco
PO Box 104
Sausalito
CA 94966-0104
Tarot Network News features the latest on tarot contacts, new developments etc. Write to the above address.

The Santa Cruz School for Tarot and Qaballah Studies
Telephone: (001) 408 423 9742.

AUSTRALIA
New Life Promotions (Australia)
Loched Bag 19
Pyrmont
NSW 2009
Telephone: 02 552 6833
Fax: 02 566 2354
For international promotions, and a wide spectrum of contacts.